Bitterness and Sweet Love: *The Way of the Cross*
and other Lenten poems

by Rita A. Simmonds

Copyright ©Rita A. Simmonds, 2014

All rights reserved

No part of this publication may be reproduced, stored in or introduced into a retrieval system, or transmitted, in any form or by any means, without the prior written permission of the copyright owner/author.

Cover photograph: by Maurizio Capuzzo
Communion and Liberation's Good Friday Way of the Cross over the Brooklyn Bridge, March 29, 2013

DEDICATION

For my loving husband
who loves the Cross of Christ

ACKNOWLEDGMENTS

These poems, some in significantly different versions, have appeared in *MAGNIFICAT* magazine: "Night Prayer," "Merciful Moon," "Bartimaeus," "Redemption," "Desert Rain," "The Transfiguration," "The Kingdom of God Belongs to Such as These," "Sacrifice," "The Killed Calf"

TABLE OF CONTENTS

I. THE WAY OF THE CROSS

- *First Station: Jesus Is Condemned to Death 2*
- *Second Station: Jesus Bears His Cross 3*
- *Third Station: Jesus Falls for the First Time 4*
- *Fourth Station: Jesus Meets His Mother 5*
- *Fifth Station: Jesus Is Helped by Simon 6*
- *Sixth Station: Veronica Wipes the Face of Jesus 7*
- *Seventh Station: Jesus Falls for the Second Time 8*
- *Eighth Station: Jesus Meets the Women of Jerusalem 9*
- *Ninth Station: Jesus Falls the Third Time 10*
- *Tenth Station: Jesus Is Stripped of His Garments 11*
- *Eleventh Station: Jesus Is Nailed to the Cross 12*
- *Twelfth Station: Jesus Dies on the Cross 13*
- *Thirteenth Station: Jesus Is Taken Down from the Cross 14*
- *Fourteenth Station: Jesus Is Laid in the Tomb 15*

I. OTHER LENTEN POEMS

- *Night Prayer 17*
- *Way of Prayer 18*
- *The Hall of Sorrow 19*
- *Merciful Moon 20*
- *Bartimaeus 21*
- *Redemption 22*
- *Desert Rain 23*
- *The Transfiguration 24*
- *The Tree of Memory 26*
- *The Kingdom of God Belongs to Such as These 27*
- *Sacrifice 28*
- *The Killed Calf 30*

The Way of the Cross

First Station: Jesus Is Condemned to Death

We look at the Man, but don't seek His Face
covered in spittle and blood that's been sweat.
The water that waits is for hands to erase
the deed that the creed will never forget.

The Man is both shepherd and lamb at the altar.
His Kingdom is silent, like seeds being sown.
The Truth is Humanity standing for slaughter.
The Way is the Life that is offered full blown.

Second Station: Jesus Bears His Cross

There is a moment
when we accept
to bear the burden
of the road.
It's that split second
when we could reasonably
curse the way
but don't.

When we say "yes" like Mary,
to the gift of the seed
birth and death happen
at once—
bitterness and sweet love.

Third Station: Jesus Falls for the First Time

What is this strange, relentless seed that falls beneath the weighty pine?
It leaves its mark upon the land in struggle to survive.
It cannot stay and swell the earth
as blow by blow though uncontrolled
will serve a firm design.
The earth is groaning for the fruit
that frees the way to die.

Fourth Station: Jesus Meets His Mother

Stay for just a moment longer.
Linger...
But the finger of time
the harshness of circumstance
demand us on.
It is not finished
yet the moment
the perfect moment
picked out of misery
is gone.
A quick glance.
A hand on a shoulder.
We move on.
Is the moment really gone?

Fifth Station: Jesus Is Helped by Simon

You
in your need
have brought shame upon me
for I am made to take your place
and keep the pace you cannot keep.

I'll take what's mine.
You take what's yours.

These strangers laugh my soul to scorn.

I cannot carry on this course.
Disgrace, take back your beam!

These scoffers scrap my soul to seed.

What have you to do with me?
Your garment's mud.
Your sweat is blood.
Your brow is twisted tree.

And me?
I'm but a passer-by
who lifts the weight and looks behind
who leaves the space of ridicule
but watches as you stumble through:

The shame that's yours is
mine.

Sixth Station: Veronica Wipes the Face of Jesus

I run to the suffering Son of Man.
Is yours the Face of God
veiled in bloodied visage
veiled again as image
that arrests my wringing hands?

Seventh Station: Jesus Falls for the Second Time

A worm.
Not a man.
Lacerated tissue.
Torn skin.
A product of our sin.

We look away
and well we should
unless we've come
to help Him stand
to bear His pain
to know the Man.

Eighth Station: Jesus Meets the Women of Jerusalem

Remember how you cried
when you saw Our Savior brutalized
along the way?
"Do not weep for me,"
you still can hear him say.

So soon the surge of evil
has brought too much to bear.
As you "weep for yourselves"
His words become clear.

How to grasp the high tide?
Where's the hand that can save?
The Body of Christ
breaks in on the wave
holding fast to the wood
as green becomes dry
the Word becomes clear,
"I'm here! Do not cry."

Ninth Station: Jesus Falls the Third Time

The Son of Man has fallen in this world.
This third time
his head hits hard against the wood.
What do his glazed eyes see
stars
galaxies
all leading back
from this narrow street
to the Father's mighty hand?
The Son has fallen
to redeem the sins of man against himself
against the Son of Man.
He rises from this earth
and goes forward
to die
momentarily forsaken
by the Father
in time.

Tenth Station: Jesus Is Stripped of His Garments

Lots are thrown.
One will win
the seamless robe
stripped with skin.
But who has owned
spattered, soaked
in Body, Blood—
the faultless cloak?

Eleventh Station: Jesus Is Nailed to the Cross

His body's been stretched to the limitless,
wrought iron holding human hands and feet.
The inscription claims this attraction is "King."
The Queen accepts.
She is strong but not steeled,
wounded by nails
her heart
to his heel.
She fights with him for life
with every labored breath.
His flesh is pressed
and spasms in her flesh.

This child she's borne has suffered, will die
yet the sorrowful mother is blessed to conceive
what hatred and haste can't fix on a tree.
The Kingdom of Love is of freedom and seed.

Twelfth Station: Jesus Dies on the Cross

A sword has slit her soul.
His blood is upon us
everywhere
in shocking overflow.
Why have You forsaken me?
rattles and rakes her spine
amplifies an echoing need.
It swirls down
to a time ago
to its long-awaiting seed.
The cry arrives.
The Spirit flies.
A Savior is conceived.
Why have You forsaken me?
At last, he breathes.
The flesh implodes.
Salvation is released.

Thirteenth Station: Jesus Is Taken Down from the Cross

What profit is there
in killing this man
who claimed to be king
who would not save himself
so lifeless he hangs on a beam?
He could not save himself
so he must be removed
from his post.
What profit is there
in a body brought down
to—Behold!
Uncoil his crown
for his mother awaits
his Kingdom come down
to enfold.

Fourteenth Station: Jesus Is Laid in the Tomb

The Word
has weight
pondered unbroken
carefully carried
quietly placed
solemnly sealed
remembered
awaited
revealed—
The Word has
weight
seeded
and sown
each step
on its own is
The Way.

Other Lenten Poems

Night Prayer
My hands were raised at night without ceasing.~Psalm 76

Nocturnal trees,
brown and bare,
you cannot pray
to everywhere,
but reach with limbs
of many roads
all ending in the unenclosed
where moonlight,
like an angel bright,
delivers Sovereign glow.

Way of Prayer

The sight of smoke
ascending
carries out
my inner space—
requests
so close
they
leave and linger
both—
to be offered
not erased.

The Hall of Sorrow

Sorrow slides
and shifts inside
the wide hall
of the heart,
walking never straight
but sober,
holding walls
that hold
the hall-marks
left behind.

Merciful Moon

Oh Softer Sun,
you have not come
to scorch
nor dry the dew.
Behold the trees!
They have no knees,
but still they worship you.
Their arms stretched high,
withholding sighs,
are bent to know the light.
Hide not your face
from hands that pray,
or feel their way through night.

Bartimaeus

Take pity on me that I may see!

Though shame seeks to bind
the throbbing impulse
that repeats its question,
paying mind
to the prodding insult
that deletes suggestion—
How to calm my nerves
when I hear the footed Word
walk by?
How to hold my tongue,
and keep His call
unsung reply?

Take pity on me that I may see!

Let my whole life's night
sing out for sight
as feet of clay
step light
by day
into the sphere
of earth
so near
my stepped on right.

Redemption

Ashes on the forehead
falling through lashes
make dusty tears
that hope to cry
to set things right,
like old and rusty errors
no effort
can affect
to forever
take from sight.

Nails will always bend
when struck
from any angle
but head-on,
and still we hammer
without light
and hope to hit
directly
correcting
darkness
with more night.

Come candle,
let hope
be not hypnotized
but heightened
in the blaze
of purest
light.

Desert Rain

With broken heart and banished life
we wait for drops of rain to cry.
This is the desert, parched terrain.
Lord, purify what will not die.

Our sin has moved our souls from self.
We wait for drops of rain to cry
in drifts of sand that shift our stance
and stall all will to try.

The desert is an arid place
that waits for drops of rain to cry.
Lord, here we seek your swollen face,
the gaze that stayed when we denied.

The desert holds your chosen race
that tasted manna from the sky.
The rain that falls is living Grace.
Lord Jesus, purify!

The Transfiguration

My master, how you die.
The lots are cast.
Your cloak is air.
Your flesh is blood,
Your face, a mirror
reflecting disbelieving stare.
There is no ghost to tell me why.
There is no voice proclaiming Truth.
The Father has forgotten you.
Elijah's gone.
And Moses too.
The hill's a deepening sigh.

Your faithful friends are losing faith.
The wind has wept all through the night.
It cannot lift a strand of cloth.
How will it raise your flesh to life?

Tabor is a memory
or merely distant dream
that left when came the agony,
that shattered when you screamed.
Brilliance turns its white to fear.
Light is shock at death.
The cross transfigures human thought,
and staggers word and breath.

Why have you forsaken me,
O Tabor that we climbed?
The face that drips in dark defeat
has drained the life of memory,
and mortified my eyes.

Coming down the mountainside,
you said that you'd arise.
Elijah came in Baptist's way
and who could recognize?
Coming down the mountainside,
a vision held our lives.
O Calvary of memory,
your hour's come: Arise!

The Tree of Memory
Standing by the cross of Jesus were His mother, and His mother's sister, Mary the wife of Clopas, and Mary Magdalene.
(Jn. 19:25)

Trees' arteries
tell the tale
of blood on wood;
capillaries
kiss cold air.
Had you been there
would you
have stood
the stretch
the tear
the nakedness,
the heartless
hollow stares?
Would you
have stood
the contradiction
in the air—
immortal body
branched
and dead
on wood?

The Kingdom of God Belongs to Such as These
(Mt. 19, 14)

Oh Lord, how well you loved the child
that died with you, the day you died.
His body was a man's, like yours;
his deeds before were like the man's
way on the other side
who could not turn himself towards life,
except to twist his head
and spit terse curses from wrinkled lips;
he seemed already old and dead.

But that child to your right
who held the place of honor,
(the place the others wanted,
but was not yours to give)
with heart of theft and stone, made flesh,
was stolen from the earth
and lifted up to die with you;
What made him hope re-birth?
The needling crown so absolute
and stark upon your head?
The tenderness in every breath
that led your mother's heart through death?
The evidence of innocence erect among the damned?
Or could he hear within your thirst
a plea his heart could understand?

His hope could not sustain repose;
Salvation hung so close.

"Dear Jesus, please, remember me
where thorns turn into gold."

Sacrifice

It was just yesterday
when the sun rose
on the memory of things
broken, trashed
and carried away,
and I had to ask
if I could still love
what couldn't last,
if there was
something other than forgetfulness
for devastating loss,
if there was someone
who could save
my heart from fraud.

And I remembered the Man
who loved to the point of absurdity:
Whose side held a lance
till all the blood and water
that waited could let go.

Real love has hung and died,
and must be carried
with panting and heavy sighs
to a cold place
where stone walls
reinforce the definitiveness
of the end.

But the true nature
of love
is human,

so it waits,
and divine,
so it rises
and lives again.

Let nothing
dam the flow of breaking love.

The Killed Calf

I had heard the rumors,
your fall from grace:
How you'd tossed
our father's fortune
to the dogs,
and now
disgraced and starving
you're making your way home.

I am the good son.
I fattened the calf
in your absence.
And now
to welcome you
our father says
it must be slain.

The little cow,
so stuffed with grain,
teeters on its legs.
For mercy's sake
it must be slain.

I killed the fattened calf for you,
though it tried to get away.
Its eyes rolled back inside its head.
It seized and cried
so wracked with pain.
(Who will know what price was paid?)

I am the good son.
At our father's word

I killed the calf
that could barely stand,
for my brother lives.

In every welcoming
there is a death.
In every home-coming,
a hidden sacrifice.
In every sacrifice,
the father's will
to forgive
and live again.

ABOUT THE AUTHOR

Rita A. Simmonds was born in Rochester, New York. She received her BA from Hofstra University and her MA from Teachers College, Columbia University. For several years, she worked for the City University of New York, teaching English as a Second Language. Simmonds is a three-time winner of the Best Original Poetry category at the annual Catholic Press Association Awards (2011, 2010, 2004), as well as a winner of numerous second and third place CPA awards. In 2012, fourteen of her poems were featured in the bestselling *MAGNIFICAT Year of Faith Companion*. In 2013, she published her first book of poems, *Souls and the City*. Her poetry appears regularly in *MAGNIFICAT*. Simmonds lives in Brooklyn, New York with her husband and two sons.